For the fierce, inspiring, supportive, most loving ladies in my life.

Text and illustrations copyright © Daniel James Clement

All rights reserved

For information visit:
http://www.facebook.com/Ameira-Beira-651019702017962/
http://www.instagram.com/ameirabeira/

ISBN: 978-0-578-51382-9

Ameira Beira

Written by: Daniel James Clement
Illustrated by: Alisa Kornilovska
Edited by: Matt Weerts

2019

Ameira Beira has a sweet hair-do.

Everywhere she goes,
people say, "Girl, your hair-do is SO cool!"

Ameira Beira feels happy when people say nice things,

so she replies,
"Hey Kiah Bo-Biah, your hair-do is SO cool too!"

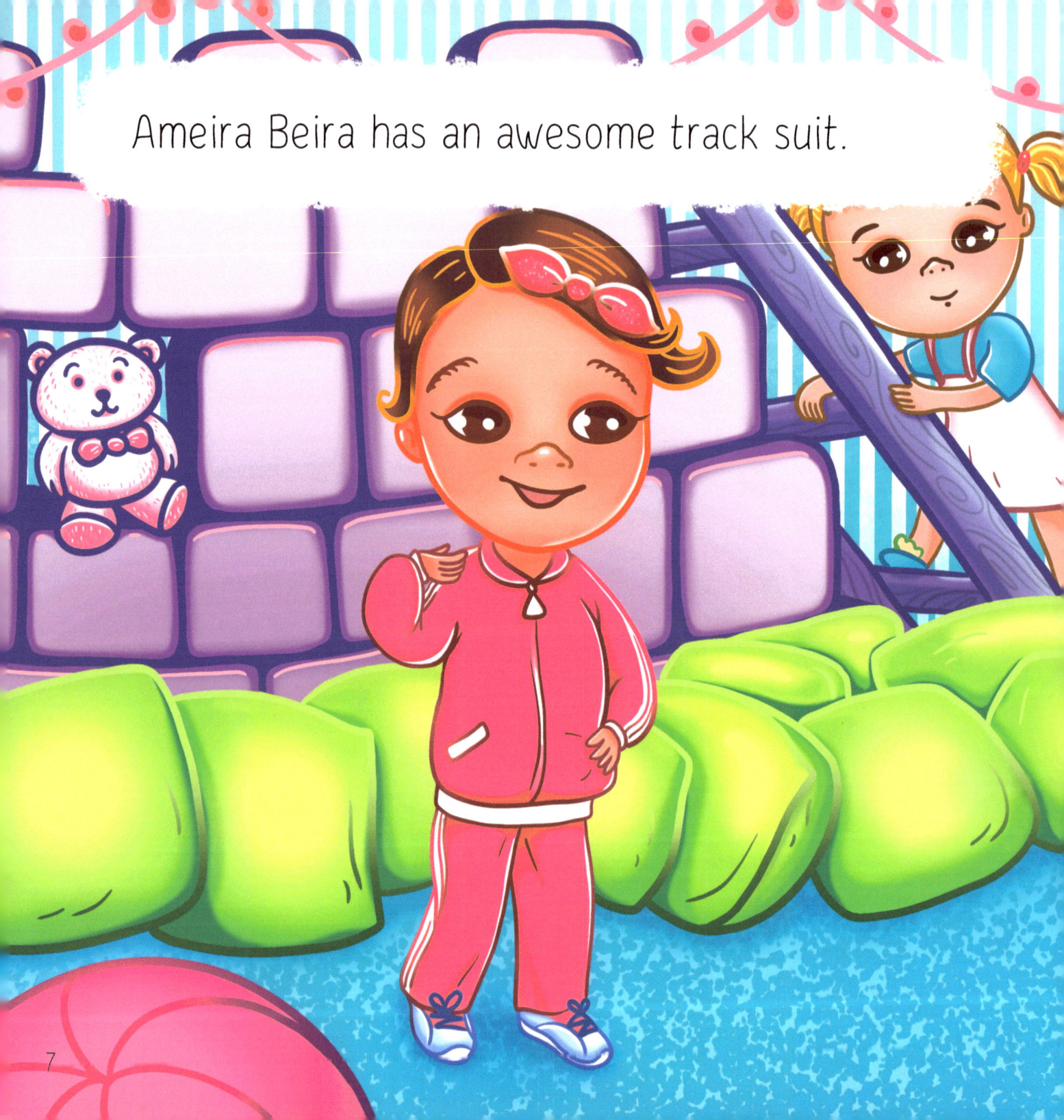
Ameira Beira has an awesome track suit.

Everywhere she goes, people say,
"Girl, your track suit is SO awesome!"

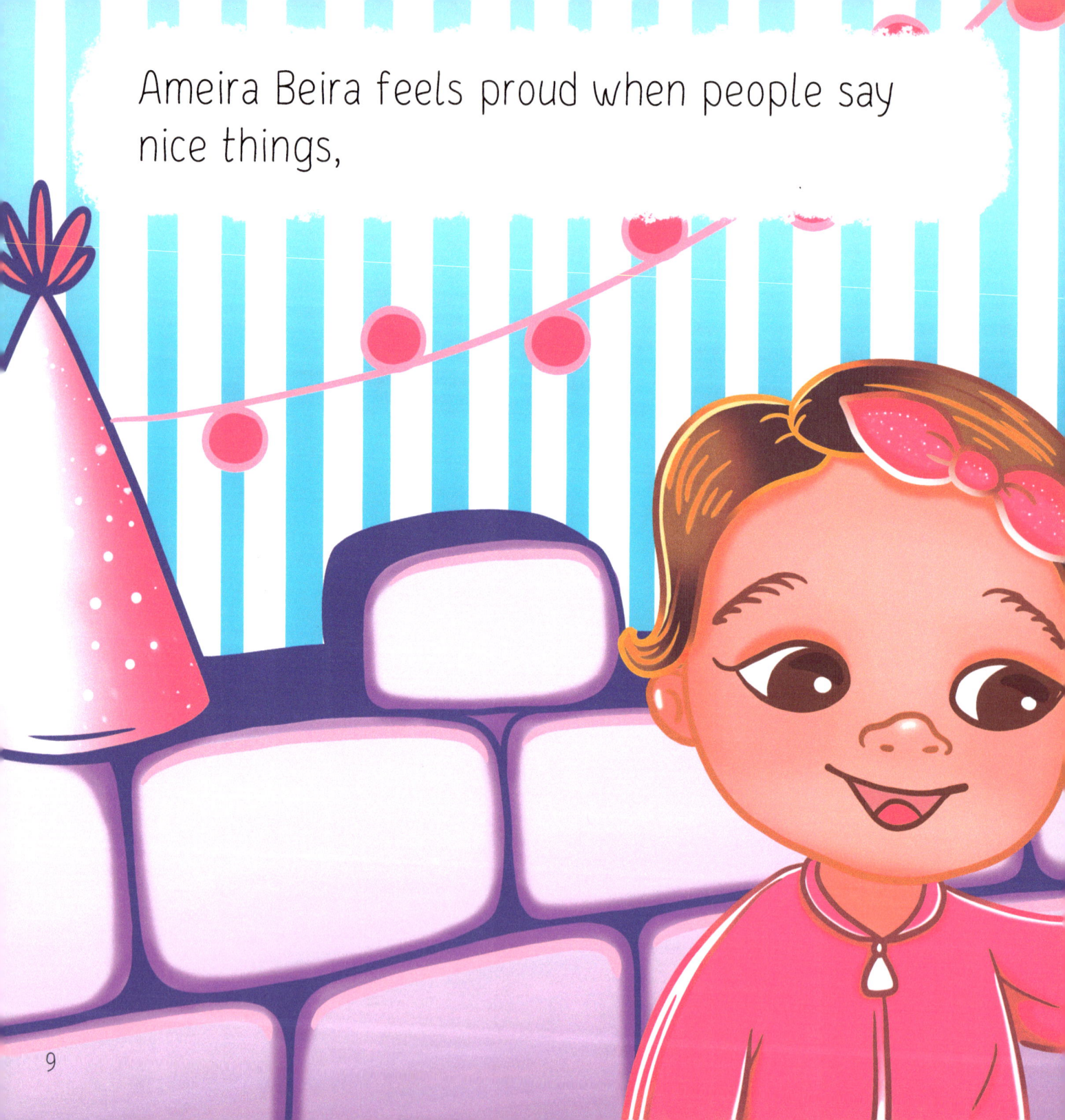

Ameira Beira feels proud when people say nice things,

so she replies, "Hey Trey Brey, your soccer uniform is SO awesome too!"

Friends

Ameira Beira is good at sports.

Everywhere she goes,
people say, "Girl, you're so good at sports!"

Ameira Beira feels empowered when people say nice things,

so she replies,
"Hey Trey Brey, you're SO good at sports too!"

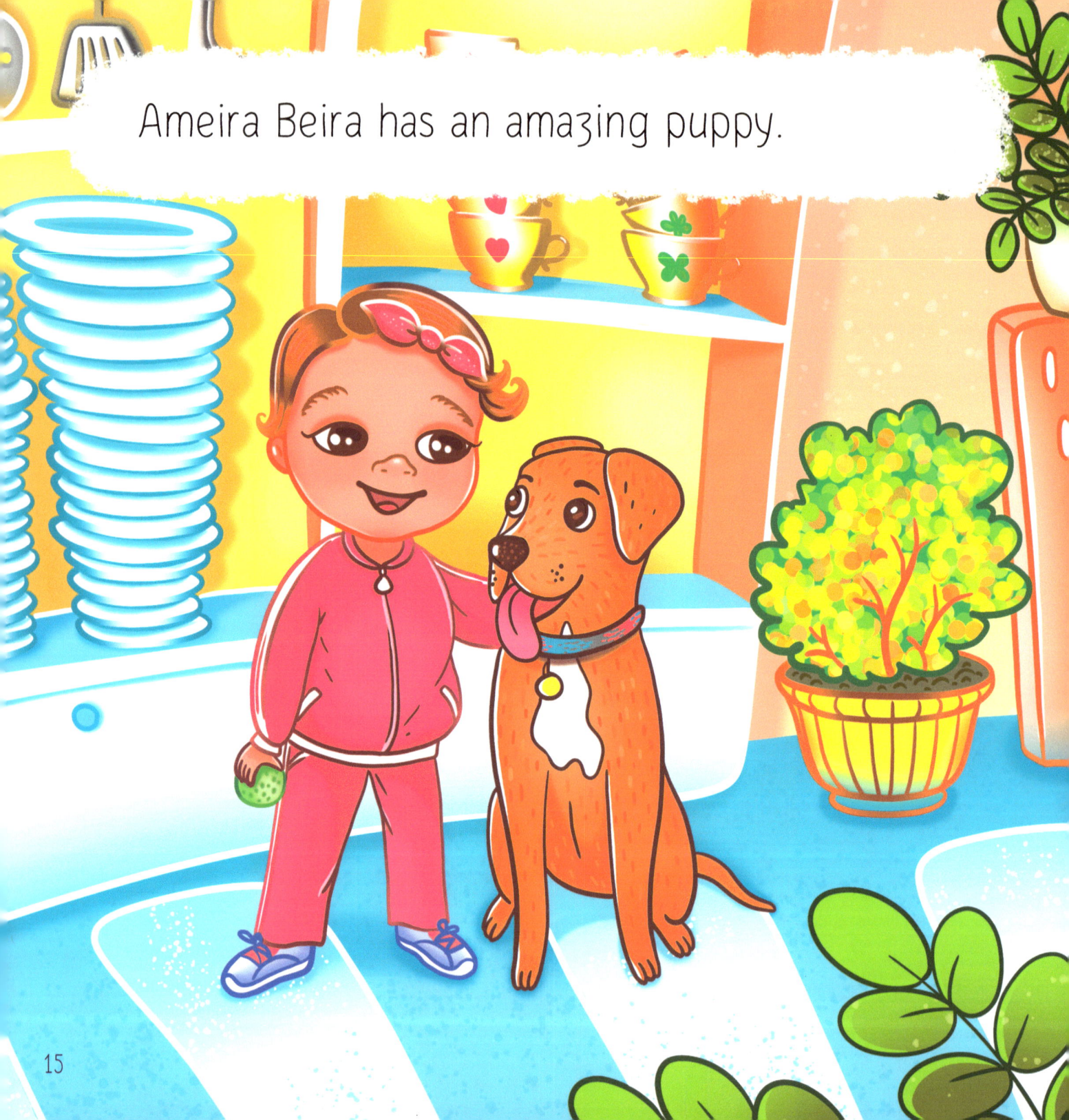

Ameira Beira has an amazing puppy.

Everywhere she goes,
people say, "Girl, your puppy is SO amazing!"

Ameira Beira feels encouraged when people say nice things, so she replies,
"Hey Lolo Bolo, your puppy is SO amazing too!"

Ameira Beira is kind and friendly.

Everywhere she goes,
people say, "Girl, you're SO kind and friendly,
and that is SO the coolest thing about you!"

Ameira Beira feels grateful when people say nice things,

so she replies, "Thanks friends, but my friends are SO the coolest thing about me!"

About the Author:
Proud Daddy 😊

www.ingramcontent.com/pod-product-compliance
Lightning Source LLC
Chambersburg PA
CBHW041155290426
44108CB00002B/74